THE MA'AT OF THE MIND

K. T. Hazine

© 2024 K. T. Hazine

Published by Hazine Publishing

All rights reserved. No part of this book may be reproduced, stored in a retrieval system, or transmitted in any form or by any means—electronic, mechanical, photocopying, recording, or otherwise—without prior written permission of the copyright holder, except for brief quotations embodied in critical reviews and certain other non-commercial uses permitted by copyright law.

For permissions requests or inquiries, please contact hazinepublishing@editorschair.com

ISBN: 978-1-0686564-1-5

Editorial Production: The Editor's Chair

Printed in United Kingdom

✯ ✯ ✯

In Loving Memory of My Late Father, Norbert Gordon Lewis

✯ ✯ ✯

Note from the Author:

As the daughter of a pastor and having studied Theology for several years, I naturally sought to follow in the footsteps of my beloved father. However, the journey to this path was not straightforward; it led me to question my faith, knowledge, and the discoveries I encountered.

Through countless late nights and early mornings of study, I have gathered morsels of information and captured striking images to illustrate my findings. While this information may not resonate with everyone, the mantra remains: "Know for yourself."

K. T. Hazine

B.A Theology

M.A Theology

M.A John Maxwell Leadership Trainer

Table of contents

01 ORDER 8

02 BALANCE 10

03 HARMONY 12

04 COMPASSION 14

05 RECIPROCITY 16

06 TRUTH 18

07 RIGHTEOUSNESS 20

08 42 LAWS NEGATIVE OF MA'AT 22

09 42 IDEALS OF MAAT 27

10	TAKEN FROM DR. MAULANA KARENGA	31
11	THE BATTLEFIELD OF THE MIND	34
12	KNOW THYSELF – FIRST	35
13	HOW DO WE KNOW OURSELVES?	36
14	THOUGHT IS FIRST	38
15	I AM THE CONSCIOUSNESS OF CHRIST	39

AS ABOVE, SO BELOW

ORDER

To arrange, organise, regulate, and classify.

To tidy, categorise, and sort out our lives.

To instruct and take charge to bid and tell,
say farewell to the god that does not do you well.

Remain Aligned With Life

BALANCE

The weighing scale, the equilibrium of balance,
a sense of peace, stability at ease.

Consider the square, calculate, compare, evaluate,
tally, and settle the scale.

Who Seeks Balance Shall Find It

HARMONY

Harmonise, complement, and correspond to bring into line.

Synchronise yet stand together.

The agreement is agreed; we walk in ancient paths.

Our Ancestors taught us: always look back.

THEY SAW, THEREFORE WE SEE

COMPASSION

The consideration of compassion in sympathy we care, your kindness and empathy I look for it there.

Out of concern our compassion is born; love and empathy being the keys of thought.

HE WHO FINDS WISDOM

RECIPROCITY

Reciprocity, like karma, turns and comes back, revisits the sender as an homecoming act.

Sent out in thought, words or deeds, our seeds yield fruit after its kind, according to its tree.

BLACK POWER

TRUTH

Truthfulness and reality reveal the facts: accuracy, precision, and exactness come back.

Dedicate your loyalty to integrity and see,
Devote legitimacy to honesty and be,
The I AM That I AM of those that created me.

SEEK TRUTH WHILE IT MAY BE FOUND

RIGHTEOUSNESS

By righteousness and justice, morality stands up.

With virtue and decency, integrity remains black.

Goodness with great principles is living the Ma'at.

SEVEN PRINCIPLES OF MA'AT

21

42 LAWS NEGATIVE OF MA'AT

1. I do nothing (ISFECTIC) wrong or evil.
2. I do nothing dishonest or underhanded.
3. My heart is not covetous.
4. I am not rapacious.
5. I do not murder human beings.
6. I do not tamper with measures or offerings.
7. I do not give short measures.
8. I do not steal divine property.
9. I do not set verbal traps.
10. I do not steal food.
11. I am not arrogant.

12. I do not go astray.

13. I do not kill the Ntru livestock.

14. I am not obstructive.

15. I do not plunder loaves which are reserved.

16. I do not gossip.

17. I do not babble.

18. I do not covet divine property.

19. I do not copulate with other men's wives or other women's husbands.

20. I am not sexually unchaste.

21. I do not inspire fear.

22. I do not consciously err.

23. My speech is not inflammatory.

24. I am not deaf towards the Ma'at – truth.

25. I do not cause uproar – turmoil.

26. I do not ignore injustice towards other people.

27. I am not jealous.

28. I do not curse or belittle other people.

29. I am not sexually abusive or oppressive.

30. I am not violent.

31. I do not become obsessed.

32. I am not hypocritical; I do not dissemble or mock the Ntru or self.

33. I am not garrulous or grabby.

34. I am not corrupt.

35. I do not curse the divine king or leader.

36. I do not wade in the water for amusement, disrupting life.

37. I do not boast.

38. I do not make people curse NTR.

39. I am not conceited.

40. I do not practice favouritism or inequity.

41. I do not magnify my credits.

42. I do not insult my local deity, Ase'.

42 IDEALS OF MA'AT

42 IDEALS OF MAAT

1. I honour with virtue.
2. I benefit with gratitude.
3. I am peaceful.
4. I respect the property of others.
5. I affirm that all life is sacred.
6. I give offerings that are genuine.
7. I live in truth.
8. I regard all altars with respect.
9. I speak with sincerity.
10. I consume only my fair share.
11. I offer words of good intent.

12. I relate in peace.
13. I honour animals with reverence.
14. I can be trusted.
15. I care for the Earth.
16. I keep my own counsel.
17. I speak positively of others.
18. I remain in balance with my emotions.
19. I am trustful in my relationships.
20. I hold purity in high esteem.
21. I spread joy.
22. I do the best I can.

23. I communicate with compassion.

24. I listen to opposing opinions.

25. I create harmony.

26. I invoke laughter.

27. I am open to love in various forms.

28. I am forgiving.

29. I am kind.

30. I act respectfully towards others.

31. I am accepting.

32. I follow my inner guidance.

33. I converse with awareness.

34. I do good.

35. I give blessings.

36. I keep the waters pure.

37. I speak with good intent.

38. I praise the Goddess and the God.

39. I am humble.

40. I achieve with integrity.

41. I advance through my own abilities.

42. I embrace the All. Ase'.

The basis of the Ten Commandments was taken from the principles of the laws of Ma'at. The principles stating 'I do not' were said in the morning, and the principles of the ideals were said in the evening or during the day, akin to what we call 'motivational statements' aimed at keeping one on the right track.

Taken from Dr. Maulana Karenga

NGUZO SABA
THE SEVEN PRINCIPLES
Swahili and English

Umoja = Unity
To strive for and maintain unity in the family, community, nation, and race.

Kujichagulia = Self-Determination
To define ourselves, name ourselves, create for ourselves, and speak for ourselves.

Ujima = Collective Work and Responsibility
To build and maintain our community together and make our brother's and sister's problems our problems and to solve them together.

Ujamaa = Cooperative Economics
To build and maintain our own stores, shops, and other businesses and to profit from them together.

Nia = Purpose
To make our collective vocation the building and developing of our community in order to restore our people to their traditional greatness.

Kuumba = Creativity
To do always as much as we can, in the way we can, in order to leave our community more beautiful and beneficial than we inherited it.

Imani = Faith
To believe with all our heart in our people, our parents, our teachers, our leaders, and the righteousness and victory of our struggle.

Three questions we should always ask ourselves:

1. Who am I?

2. Am I really who I say I am?

3. Am I all I ought to be?

The answers should guide our pathway to be true to ourselves.

THE BATTLEFIELD OF THE MIND

The mind is a battlefield where all wars take place.

The wars of entertainment, excessiveness, and fate.
The war of laziness towards the word of truth.

The battle of control spills over on the earth.
Take it spiritually by force, not carnal, you see.

Strongholds that ride through, break at the knees.

With the Almighty on your side and still on the throne,
you don't need to fear; you're not alone.

The mind is a battlefield, always wanting to take you down.

But the power we possess is holy, pure, the best.
The enemy mind cannot stand against the force of the Creator.

Your confession of Ma'at is destruction to its kingdom; they know that their time is short, and their end will soon come. They know that the sons of the valley will rule back Ma'at.

KNOW THYSELF – FIRST

Knowledge begets knowledge. The first knowledge to seek is of self. For without knowing oneself, one continues to stumble in the dark, living life by chance and mishaps. At times, things will appear as though they came into being by the power of belief in another source outside of self, or through a combined effort, accepted wisdom of prayer, meditation, deliberate thinking, planning, concept, and inspiration, to name a few. As mankind in the majority has not been taught that there's power in knowing thyself first, we give our greatness away, not understanding that the power within or the thinking within reflects without. The statement 'so a man thinketh, so is he' is true in every sense of itself. We cannot dream of greatness without applying action and expect it to fall into our laps. A tree follows the seed. There is no other way. Apple seeds will never produce grapevines, and so with the power of the mind, the seed you sow will bear the fruit that grows. The secret thoughts will manifest openly, sometimes to our downfall. It will show up as an unconscious bias or behaviour, as a change in attitude, as anger, as love, as regret, as peace, or war with self and others. Regardless, it will expose you.

HOW DO WE KNOW OURSELVES?

Firstly, let's understand what it means to know:

- ⌘ To be acquainted with
- ⌘ To be familiar with
- ⌘ To be on familiar terms with
- ⌘ To recognise
- ⌘ To identify
- ⌘ To be knowledgeable about
- ⌘ To experience

Each of the above relates to how personal self-knowledge is. We might believe we know ourselves and know without a shadow of a doubt how we would react in any given situation, but I can guarantee you your reaction can surprise even you! The mind has its own mind; its mode of operation operates in an intelligence of psyche power untapped by modern-day man.

Those who have some knowledge of the mind have tried in every way to contain it. However, the mind works in harmony with the universe and therefore it cannot be totally contained. There is a mind of the universe, a creative mind that does not sleep or slumber, that takes all thoughts, actions, and all spoken words into the creative realm to reproduce them. The universal mind does not have the knowledge of right or wrong; it just reacts. Mankind can also amalgamate in thought to change or alter circumstances. If only we had the true knowledge of the power of agreement; it is stated that 'if two shall agree touching anything on earth, it shall be established'. Two agreeing, touching, plus the universe moving into action on your behalf is immeasurable. The power of the predetermined thought can virtually move mountains. As thoughts come into existence, the reality becomes the thought. Through meditation, visual imaging, and thought projection, it repeatedly produces after its kind. The saying 'be careful what you ask for, as you might get it' relates also to thought; thought is first.

THOUGHT IS FIRST

In the beginning was the word; the word had to be thought of first to stimulate and set into motion the authenticity of the word. We do not arrive at any given situation without previous thought because the mind, in its voracity, has the intelligence and power to amass information from lifetimes ago. Many people do not subscribe to the idea of past lives; however, if we believe we are spirit beings first living a human experience and are of the notion that spirits are non-matter, then our spirit being does not have the capacity to die as we know it. It is with this suggestion that we can start to probe the matter or thought of past lives. According to our beliefs, knowledge, and comprehension, we approach this matter either already with made-up minds or a willingness to learn and be open to new information. Accepting new information away from tradition is a difficult mindset to change. But in order to move with the new flow of mankind's evolution, we need to explore outside the boxes we have been allocated. Are we old souls, old spirits, that come back in a new dimension? That is the multi-million-pound question.

I AM THE CONSCIOUSNESS OF CHRIST

In presenting this concept, we explore an alternative perspective on studying the Bible and its terminology. We approach this from the viewpoint that the Bible was not exclusively delivered to a group universally known as the Jews. Rather, we consider that its contents comprise a collection of writings originating from thousands of years before the emergence of the Jewish people as a distinct community. These texts were later personified and set within a historical framework, exemplified by an individual named Jesus, bestowed with the title of Christ.

This approach arises from the grim reality of mankind's history, marked by torment, persecution, incineration, brutality, and dehumanisation. Faced with such horrors, individuals often conformed and embraced this doctrine out of sheer necessity to survive. They had little choice but to acquiesce to avoid suffering.

In this context, people grasped onto this narrative as a profound mystical event, perpetually seeking salvation from the perceived terrors of hell, their own sins, and the spectre of the devil lurking ominously in the background. It's essential to recognise that the English language itself, in its everyday expressions and speech patterns, has the inherent capacity to cast spells or influence perceptions, often referred to as 'spelling'.

These authors, however, were not merely mystics or individuals who feared God, and in some cases, may not have truly known God. Instead, they possessed profound psychological insights, understanding that fear could be harnessed to control others. They skilfully crafted a narrative that exploited the human fear of a punishing afterlife for those who failed to adhere to the prescribed instructions. Yet, intriguingly, these same institutions that wielded wickedness upon mankind often appeared to lack fear of the very God they preached about—an unsettling contradiction encapsulated by the phrase 'wickedness in high places'.

The real interpretation is not of a saviour coming from the sky but of Man and the soul of Man, a hidden message that only a seeker would find—those looking for the whole truth and having an open mind. The Bible tells us, 'Kings search out a matter'; after seeking truth, one should be fully initiated into research and investigation. The findings can lead to one of two discussions: go back to what you have been subjective to or face the reality of the matter, that you played no part in except to be open and willing to learn. The truth can be used to its full advantage for the greatness of mankind or used to control and manipulate mankind through fear. As the quote says, 'the mind is a beautiful thing to waste'; knowing the power of the mind, thoughtfulness, and the subconscious mind, these men fully understood that if man was left to use it, they wouldn't be able to control mankind. Again, as the saying goes, 'what is hidden must come to light' and 'there's a season for every purpose under heaven'. Exposure is a divine purpose. Don't get me wrong; quite a great message is revealed in the Bible, and principles that are undeniable laws from the Creator. It's the totality of the personification of believing that you are not your own saviour, and to even think it, much less speak it, is blaspheming.

Signs, symbols, codes, and twisted clues are rampant throughout the Bible. If only we would do as the Bible says, 'study to show yourself approved, rightly dividing the word'. Reading and learning all come down to interpretation and research if we were not so captivated by the fairy tale of it. In Sunday school, we are taught Bible stories. Surely, we understand that a story is made up to entertain. Unfortunately, for some of us, we have been taught the lie for so long that nothing someone else says would allow the believer to even think that the stories of the Bible have any possibility they could have been stolen and rewritten for the masters' benefit, and not from the spoken word from God to man. Most just wouldn't be able to handle it because now you'll have to let go of the notion of being saved and the falsity of the burning pit of hell and brimstone for eternity. In many cultures, hell is a concept that was given by others—the predator, the slave masters, and the saviour look very much alike. Well done, con.

The quotation 'change your mind, change your life' means taking back control over yourselves. It's about taking full responsibility for your actions, thoughts, and outcomes. You become or have whatever you think of most of the time. From within manifestation to outside materialisation, the Bible tells you to 'think on these things: whatsoever is good, true, and of good report'. Instead, we are fighting a devil or demon of some kind, blaming things outside of ourselves for decisions we made, giving away our God-given power. Another quote from the Bible, 'out of the abundance of the heart, the mouth speaks'. The mouth reveals the thoughts, and the body exposes the true person. These are principles and laws that cannot be broken. What goes up must come down, what you sow you must definitely reap. Man thinking of himself as one with God is right thinking. The Bible states, 'I and the Father are one'. If the hidden interpretation is on a conscious level, you are one with your consciousness. You are the creator of your said desire, and the Father is the expression or sub-consciousness of your inward thinking. So yes, you're one and the same. Consciousness brings forth whatever you hold in mind long enough, so to change what you possess externally, you must change what you're creating mentally. The saying 'The kingdom is within you' comes to mind. The mind has no limits on it; its only limits are the ones we have caged ourselves to. We look at our surroundings, our lives, our parents, and friends, and most of us can't imagine a limitless life—a life of anything and everything we can say or think of.

Should mankind live from the understanding that the kingdom of God is within you, the kingdom being a mindset that you're in total control of, the higher self could be considered as the kingdom of thoughts. As you decree, such has been given unto you. The Bible says 'just believe', and with belief, you draw the magnifications of your desires.

Using the idea of prayer works in much the same way. The Bible tells you to 'go inside your closet and pray in secret, and he who hears will reward you openly'. Now, could the secret place be your subconscious thinking? Because remember, 'thoughts become things', so whether you speak it out or pray, it acts as the same thing. Thoughts have the energy to go out into the atmosphere, so be careful of what you wish for; you just might get it! The undeniable principle of this law is impersonal and has no regard for anyone; it will come to pass.

The secret of the psychological form of the written word was so constructed and instituted to contain the mind of mankind in a series of 'stories' and mystical events, evading the true mysteries and spiritual rituals that our ancestors performed. Instead, we were given a form of historical events and belief in it is a hidden code of laws and principles that the unread and fearful person in the occults wouldn't have a clue about. Hence, man has been and is still taught to praise, worship, and look entirely outside of self for power and manifestations of what he wants to achieve.

The readers of the Bible are totally unaware of the symbolic language and codes, fully believing that the characters were actual living people, not recognising them as a well-written and rehearsed fabrication. Only when man comes to the reality of the true interpretations of the 'written word' and its association with the consciousness of self and his mind, will he avoid being deceived. Most of mankind is so indoctrinated with the biblical majesty of God that they are unwilling to claim what the Bible tells them: 'You are made in the image and likeness of God, and that you can do all things.' The operative word here is 'you', not negating the Creator of all things but understanding that 'you' can! If you are made in the image and likeness, it's saying that you are a reflection of whom or what you're representing. Why? Because it also tells us 'Ye are Gods.' Moses did try to help the reader by declaring, 'The I Am sent me.' The I AM—in other words, the Me sent Me!

Although it's written over and over again in plain sight, we seem to overthink it, making it really deep and focusing on the outside of self. So, when you read:

- ⌘ I AM THE LIGHT
- ⌘ I AM THE WAY
- ⌘ I AM THE TRUTH
- ⌘ I AM THE BEGINNING AND THE ENDING

The statement is really directed towards oneself, not the other way around. You are speaking to yourself first; I Am is you speaking or addressing yourself. I Am is not a name. So when 'Moses' was speaking, he was actually saying, 'I AM' or 'I HAVE' has come to see about the matter. He had decided consciously before going to show up physically. This is the Father and the Son as one. The subconscious and conscious minds working as one, the thought and it being fulfilled through the action. This can also be interpreted as heaven meeting earth, where heaven is your higher self and earth is your lower self. Scriptures tell us, 'Be still and know that I am God.' Being still means being quiet and knowing that 'I am God.' This again points to the self, which is a major impossibility for many Christians to comprehend. They don't realise it's the same as setting your mind on a mission and staying focused on what you want to achieve, and surely you'll reap the benefits.

'I and God are one; I and my conscious self are one of the same. I cannot be without my consciousness; I cannot do anything without first having a conscious thought.' What you think of, you become or have. You express your deepest desires primarily through your conscious thought state. Statements like these fool people into thinking that the Father is outside of us. But with the understanding of the Father as the subconscious and the Son as the awareness or conscious, knowing this principle, the Father is the higher self. The Father comes before the Son.

In plain sight, 'The Kingdom of God is Within You.' The Bible here is telling us the whole truth—the kingdom of God is within. The kingdom is the higher self, and Jesus is the lower self or lower consciousness. It is written, 'I can do nothing by myself, I go to the Father.' Going to the Father is taking off all limits, pulling out all the stops to make 'all things possible to them that believe'. How magnificent is the Creator? One has to be drawn by the Father, your higher self, before you can bring into reality the thought desire of the lower self or the Son. This is hidden in plain sight from the world. It is told to you, but then the truth of the meaning is given a different concept. The real meaning empowers man himself, while the lie makes man void of power, depending on a falsity.

The preparation before praying is having or going into your secret place. You are told to close the door and as you pray, believe in what you are asking for, to the point of already possessing it. Since the mind doesn't distinguish between truth and reality, you are to 'fake it until you make it' or have it. This is how 'all things are possible'. We have been taught to believe that 'Jesus' is the giver of all things, not understanding that we have brought things into being with our belief. In other words, 'what we've asked for in secret, we shall be rewarded openly by your Father who abides in secret'. Again, this prayer expresses the working of two minds. Whatever you desire or think about constantly in your secret place, which is also your mind where it's created in the first place, becomes your reality.

This act of a desired prayer and belief is the same as you as the Father, consciousness, and the Son, the audible or experienced outcome. From within becomes without. Once we understand that opening our minds to the greatness we truly are, we'll know without a shadow of a doubt that we are the creators of our heaven and hell. Remember, thoughts become things. Anything! Whatever is said silently or secretly, whatever is uttered, is picked up by the atmosphere and goes to work to bring it into existence. The atmosphere believes it's helping you to achieve your desire because that's what it's constantly hearing from you.

The power of the mind is a fascinating subject.

Question: What is the mind?

Answer: The mind is a powerhouse that each individual has in their control. In other words, we are masters of our mind and should have complete control of it. Statements such as:

- ⌘ You are what you think.
- ⌘ You are where you are because of what you thought yesterday.
- ⌘ Your words define or condemn you.
- ⌘ Control your tongue and your thoughts, and you will control your life.
- ⌘ What you sow is what you will reap—farmers don't sow corn and expect mangoes.
- ⌘ Thoughts become things.
- ⌘ Think greatness to be great.
- ⌘ Thoughts of poverty and lack give you just that—poverty and lack.

⌘ Imaginations make pictures—pictures make life.

⌘ Picture it to live it.

⌘ If you can touch it in your mind, you'll hold it in your hands.

⌘ Live the best dream.

⌘ Only I have total control of my mind.

⌘ Don't let anyone walk through your mind with dirty boots.

This must be our ongoing thinking. The saying 'if you stand for nothing, you'll fall for anything' also works with the way you allow garbage into your mind.

The mind is the organ that controls the entire body. You can have a hole in your heart and live a nearly normal life, but some of us act as though we have a hole in our brain because we operate at less than a quarter per cent of our potential. Why? Why have we allowed the master computer that the Almighty has given us to lay waste? Is it laziness, slothfulness, or sluggishness, or is it fear? Each one of us must answer this question for ourselves. What is it that holds us back? What happened? For some of us, it is who happened to us. Why did someone else have to leave, die, remarry, move abroad—the list is endless as to why someone else did something that we are not in control of. That's our 'get out of jail card'. We blame everyone first, but we must face the unbearable truth, which is that the 'buck starts and stops here'. Am I a blamer, or do I not hold anyone responsible for where I am or how my life is? I have to be mature enough to take full accountability, regardless of whether I liked the outcome or not. How we react to what attacks us determines how our mind receives it and then perceives what has happened. Life happens, and sometimes, blocks are created in the mind, and people get stuck.

But the Almighty created us to re-create. Think of the wonders of the world, and the Almighty still expects us to re-create and increase knowledge on the earth. We have taken the world so much for granted that we have closed down areas of our brain, so we are operating in survival mode and don't even know it. The world media has anesthetised the brains of people and created its own version of individuals instead. They tell you when and how to think, what to think, and even whether to think! Situations happen, and the bombardment of lies that is fed to the public paralyses the mind with fear because the general public believes in the media. They genuinely believe that 'those who rule' care about them. I suppose, on the deepest level, no one wants to admit that those who care for them are really their enemies. So, the deceit continues, and people are continually led astray.

Question: Why do you think people are misled?

People are being misled and miseducated out of fear. Those who rule the world aim to bring in the New World Order, with control over the people, the atmosphere, and the land. They leave the people wanting, and the rulers want to be seen as the saviours of the world.

What kind of God would allow man to destroy another and pray for forgiveness and repeat it over and over again? That's not a loving God. That's a wicked man.

The Works of the Almighty Creator

www.ingramcontent.com/pod-product-compliance
Lightning Source LLC
Chambersburg PA
CBHW050855010526

44118CB00004BA/167